Hands-On Projects

CIRCUS

Active Learning about the Arts

by Carol Wawrychuk & Cherie McSweeney
illustrated by Philip Chalk

Contents

Introduction	3
Big Top	4
Baby Elephant	6
Sawhorse Pony & Carriage	8
Vendor Hat	13
Vendor Tray	15
Cotton Candy	16
Clown Shirt	17
Clown Bow Tie	18
Clown Hat	20
Tightrope Walker Pole	21
Tightrope Wristbands	22
Tightrope Walker Hat	23
Ringmaster Vest	24
Ringmaster Hat	25
Clown with Growing Hair	26
Elephant Puppet	28
Paper Plate Lion Mask	30
Paper Bag Tiger Puppet	31
Dancing Bear and Stand	33
Counting Circus Bears	36
Circus Playdough	40
Circus Flannel Board	41
Clown Matching Activity	43
Circus Puzzle	45
Circus Memory Match	47

Lovingly dedicated to Katie McSweeney and Todd Wawrychuk
for their child-like inspirations.

Entire contents copyright ©1998 by Monday Morning Books, Inc.
For a complete catalog, please write to the address below:
P.O. Box 1680
Palo Alto, CA 94302 U.S.A.

Call us at: 1-800-255-6049
E-mail us at: MMBooks@aol.com
Visit our Web site:
http://www.mondaymorningbooks.com

Monday Morning is a registered trademark of
Monday Morning Books, Inc.

monday morning.

Permission is hereby granted to reproduce student materials in this book for
non-commercial individual or classroom use.
ISBN 1-57612-039-2
Printed in the United States of America
987654321

Circus ©1998 Monday Morning Books, Inc.

Introduction

The circus is coming to town! *Circus* is a thematic unit in which children make a big top using butcher paper, cardboard tubes, and paint. Once the tent is made, the magic unfolds. The ringmaster and tightrope walker "ride" into the arena in an appliance box carriage pulled by an elegant sawhorse pony. Awaiting them is a life-size baby elephant created from boxes, coffee cans, buttons, and an old gray sock. Paper bags, paper plates, file folders, and old T-shirts are transformed into dramatic play props for a clown, ringmaster, and tightrope walker. The children dress in vendors' costumes to sell "cotton candy" made from colored cotton balls. Animal puppets and masks spark their imaginations as they interact with one another.

All of the colors, shapes, and animals of the circus provide an excellent opportunity for matching, sorting, and recognition activities to challenge the young learner.

Personal Observations:

While making the big top, children discussed visiting the circus. They could hardly wait to put the finishing touches on the baby elephant, and many asked if they could bring in grass or peanuts for him to eat. Conversations between the baby elephant and the elephant puppets were ongoing. The roars of lion and tiger puppets echoed throughout the room.

Once the tent and props were completed, the children became engaged in dramatic play. They exchanged costumes during this time, so everyone got a turn to play the different roles.

There was much excitement among the children when the clown's grass hair started to grow. This led to discussions on seed growth and the life cycle of plants.

As the children became involved in the matching, counting, sequencing, and playdough activities, they had many opportunities to interact with one another. The dramatic play experiences strengthened their eagerness to work cooperatively.

After participating in these activities, the children felt as if they were a part of the circus. Now you can open the pages of this book and watch the big top come to life!

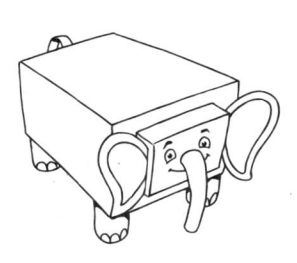

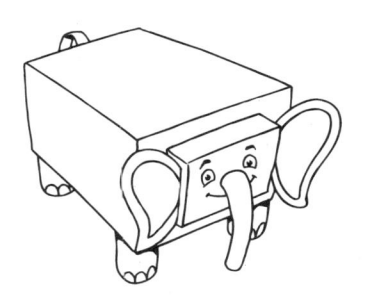

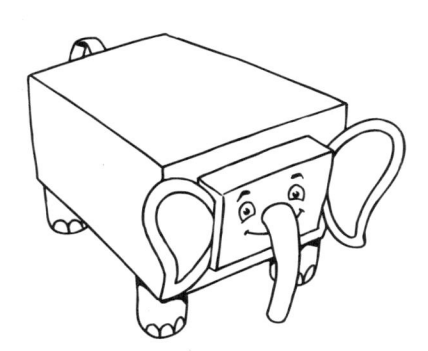

Big Top

Materials:
Four computer paper boxes (or other boxes), twelve wrapping paper tubes (or other cardboard tubes), butcher paper, masking tape, tempera paint (in assorted colors), shallow tins (for paint), paintbrushes or sponges, holiday garland, sharp instrument for cutting (for adult use only)

Directions:
1. Cut a hole in the lid and in the bottom of each computer paper box. The holes should be just large enough to fit a wrapping paper tube. (Make sure the holes are aligned on top and bottom.)
2. Connect three wrapping paper tubes by inserting one inside another. Reinforce joining sections of the pole by wrapping with masking tape. Repeat this step for the remaining tubes.
3. Cut two slits in one end of each of the long poles.

Big Top

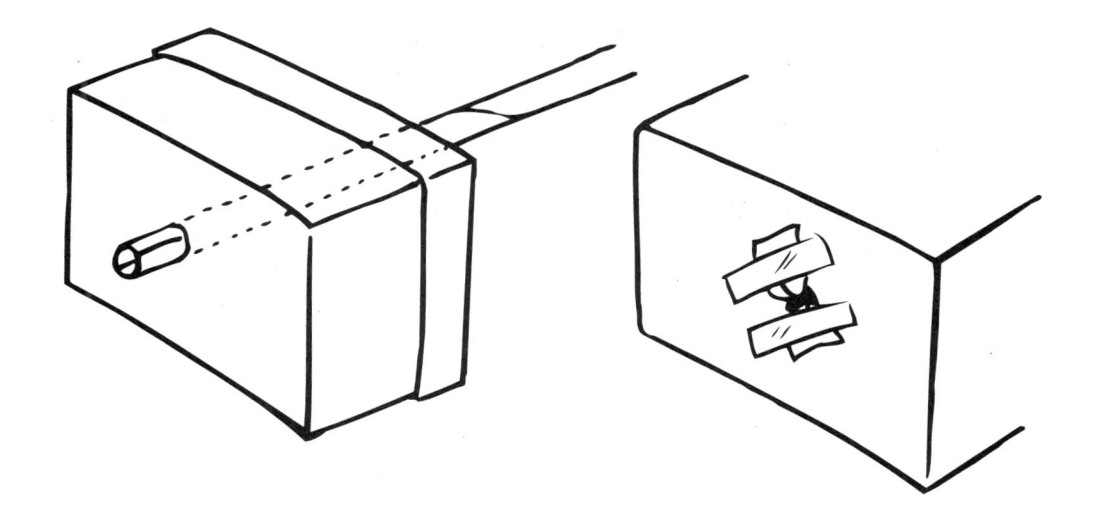

4. Insert the slit end of one pole into each box, and push the poles through both holes.
5. Spread the flaps of each pole open and tape to the bottom of the box (as shown).
6. Reinforce each pole on the top of each box with masking tape, and cover with a length of the garland.
7. Cut 18 in/46 cm wide butcher paper to the desired big top size, and scallop one edge of the paper.
8. Have children dip brushes or sponges in the tempera paint and decorate the paper.
9. Once the paint has dried, attach the big top to the poles with masking tape.

Options:
- Provide toy cars for children to dip into the paint and use to "roller paint" the butcher paper.
- Fill plastic bags with sand. Put the bags inside the boxes before inserting the poles. These will serve as weights to keep the boxes steady.

Book Links:
- *the circus* by dick bruna (Follett)
- *Circus* by Peter Spiers (Doubleday)

Baby Elephant

Materials:
Large box (the size of a two-drawer file cabinet), computer paper box without lid, four 39 oz (1.10 kg) coffee cans or large cylinder oatmeal containers, flat piece of cardboard, white paper, marker, masking tape, heavy string or yarn, long gray sock, newspaper, rubber band, plastic juice lids or buttons, glue, tempera paint (black and white), paintbrushes or sponge brushes, shallow tins (for paint), sharp instrument for cutting (for adult use only)

Directions:
1. Connect the computer paper box to the large box by poking matching holes in several places and tying with yarn.
2. Tape the flaps of the larger box closed.
3. Cut a slit in the front and on each side of the computer paper box.

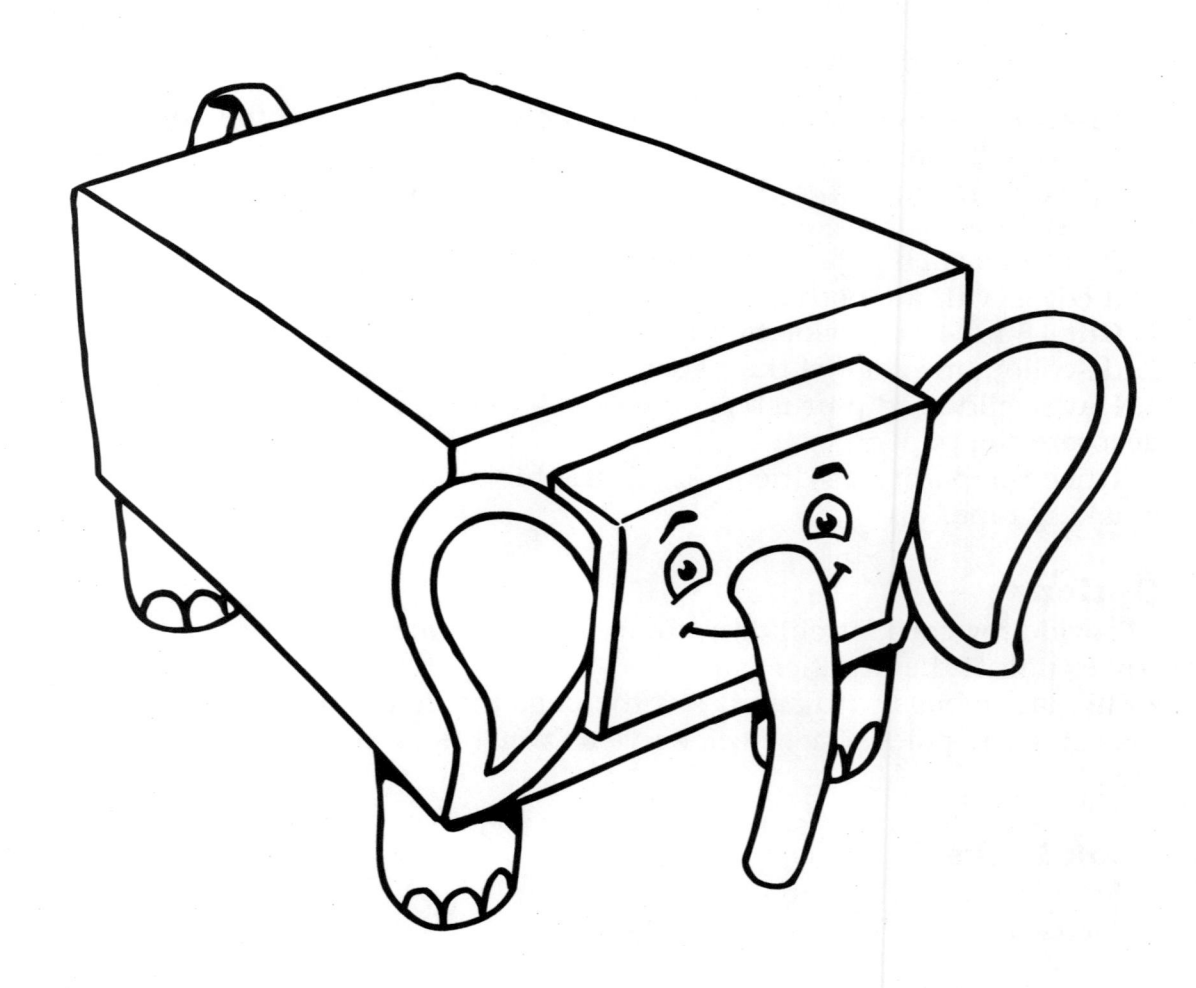

Baby Elephant

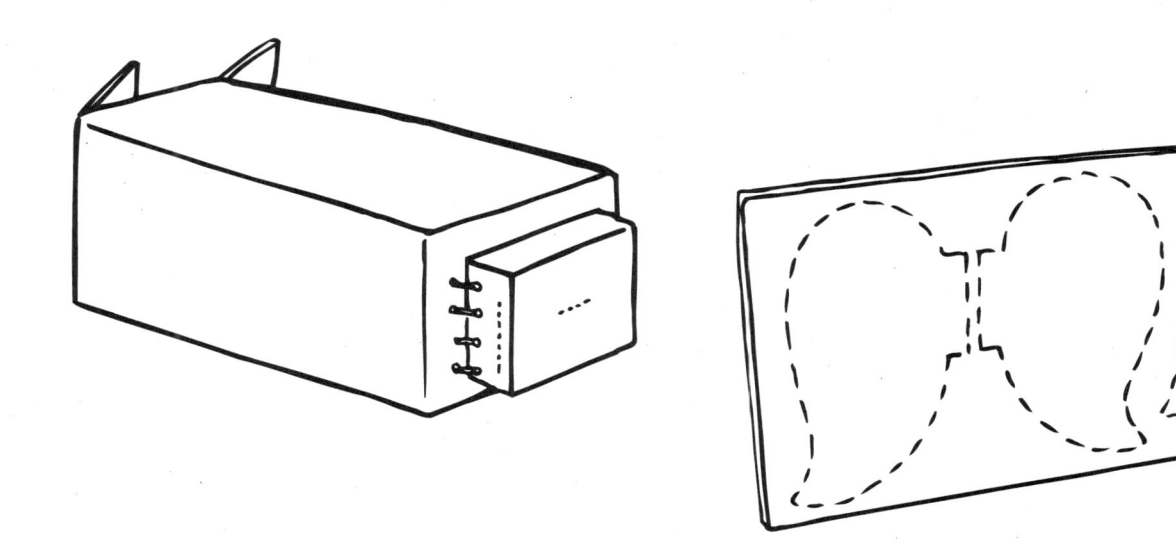

4. Cut a tail and two elephant ears from a flat piece of cardboard. (Make a tab on the ears to insert into the box.)
5. Cover the coffee cans with white paper.
6. Glue the four coffee cans onto the bottom of the box for legs, and reinforce with masking tape.
7. Have the children stuff the sock with crinkled newspaper, and secure the end with a rubber band.
8. Insert the ears and trunk in the slits, and tape the tail to the back.
9. Let the children mix black and white tempera paint together to make gray paint.
10. Provide paintbrushes or sponge brushes for children to use to paint the elephant. They can paint both the body and the face.
11. Once the paint has dried, glue plastic juice lids or buttons to the face for the eyes and nostrils.

Option:
- Highlight the ears and feet with darker gray paint, or with pink paint.

Book Links:
- *Ella* by Bill Peet (Houghton Mifflin)
- *Elmer* by David McKee (Lothrop, Lee & Shepard)

Sawhorse Pony & Carriage

Materials:
Pony Head Patterns (pp. 10-11), sawhorse, large box, white construction paper, tape, tissue or crepe paper (white, blue, and pink), sturdy paper, cardboard, tempera paint (white, black, pink, and purple), shallow tins (for paint), paintbrushes, marker, sequins, large buttons, holiday garland, heavy string or yarn, scissors, stapler, glue and glue stick, sharp instrument for cutting (for adult use only), hammer and nails (for adult use only)

Directions for Sawhorse Pony:
1. Cut sawhorse to height that allows children to sit on it safely.
2. Duplicate the pony head pattern and cut out. Attach the two halves of the pattern using tape.
3. On the flat piece of cardboard, trace the pony head pattern twice and cut out.
4. Cut a notch in the pony neck to allow for the sawhorse legs.
5. Nail the heads on both sides of the sawhorse, tying them together around the ear with yarn.

Sawhorse Pony & Carriage

6. Cut four hooves out of sturdy paper according to the diagram below.

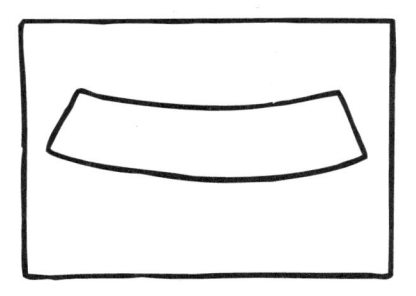

7. Have the children paint the pony white.
8. Once the paint has dried, add the facial features with black and pink paint.
9. Glue on large buttons for the pony's pupils.
10. Cut long strips of tissue or crepe paper for the children to glue to the pony's mane and tail.
11. Children can glue sequins to the pony's hooves.
12. Once the hooves are dry, wrap them around the pony's legs and staple.

Note: See "Tightrope Walker Hat" (p. 23) for directions to make the pony's headband.

Pony Head Pattern

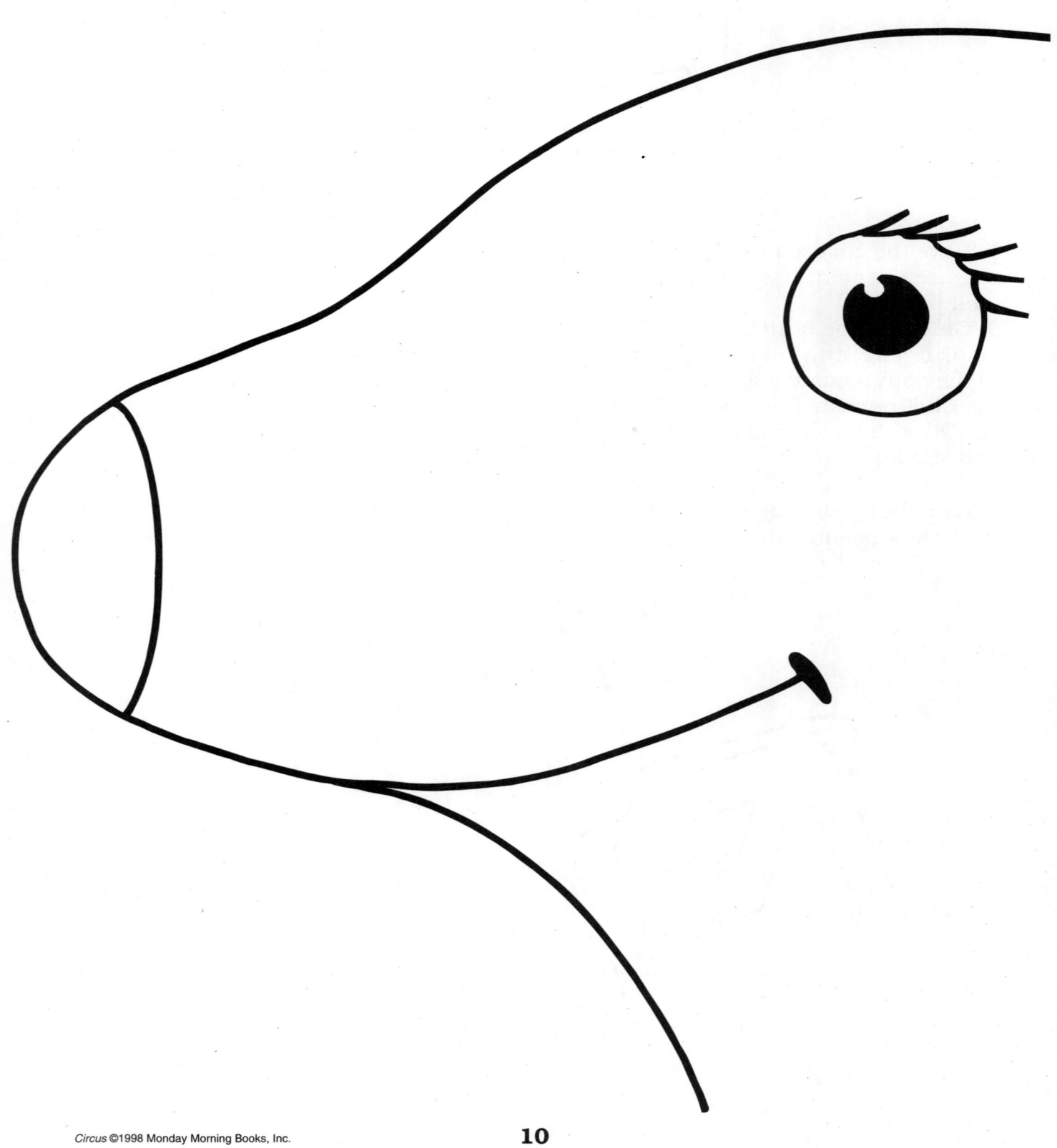

10

Pony Head Pattern

Sawhorse Pony & Carriage

Directions for Carriage:
1. Remove one side of the box.
2. Poke holes in the end flaps, and secure with heavy string or yarn.
3. Cut two sides of the box and a hole for the garland, according to the diagram below.

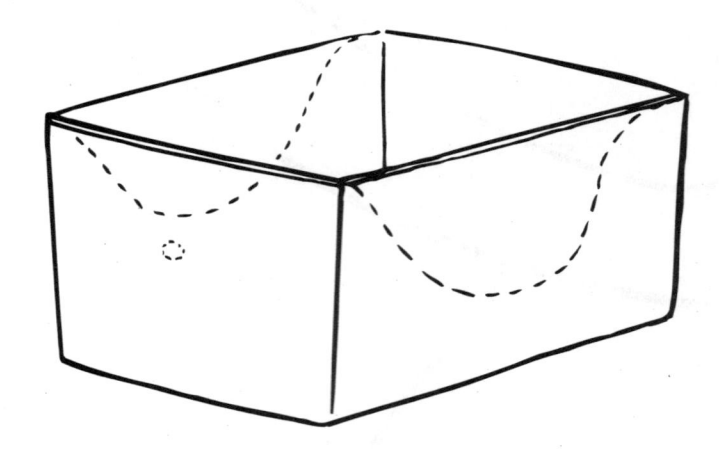

4. Cut four wheels with spokes from white construction paper.
5. Have children paint the carriage purple.
6. Once the purple paint has dried, have children use paintbrushes to splatter pink paint on the carriage.
7. Children can glue the wheels onto the dried carriage.
8. Wrap the garland around the pony's head, and bring through the hole in the carriage.

Option:
• Large wooden blocks or small chairs can be placed inside the carriage to serve as seats.

Book Links:
• *Carousel Round and Round* by Kay Chorao (Clarion Books)
• *Carnival* by M. C. Helldorfer (Viking)

Vendor Hat

Materials:
Vendor Hat Pattern (p. 14), sturdy paper or old file folder, scissors, self-sticking dots (pink, yellow, and green), elastic, crayons or markers, hole punch

Directions for One Hat:
1. Trace the hat pattern onto sturdy paper and cut out.
2. Place a self-sticking dot at each dot on the brim and punch a hole in each dot.
3. Tie a piece of elastic through each hole, and tie the loose ends together.
4. Label the cone as shown ("Cotton Candy").
5. Provide crayons, markers, and stickers for children to use to decorate the hat.
6. Once the brim is placed on a child's head, the "Cotton Candy" cone will stand up.

Video Link:
• *Spot Goes to the Circus* (Walt Disney Home Video)

Vendor Hat Pattern

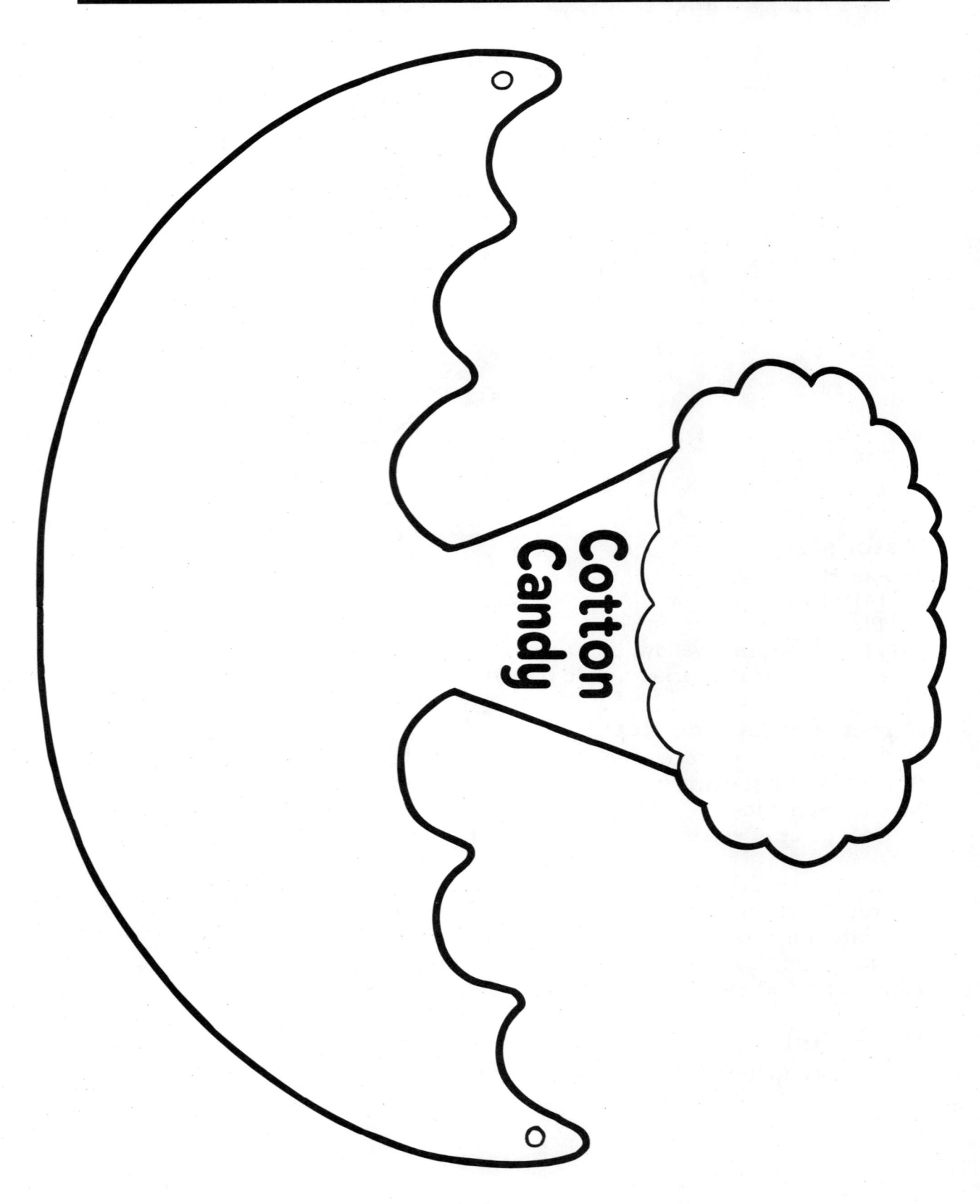

Cotton Candy

Vendor Tray

Materials:
Case-size beverage carton, yarn or cotton rope, tempera paint, shallow tins (for paint), paintbrushes, marker, sharp instrument for cutting (for adult use only)

Directions:
1. Poke one hole in the middle of each of the short sides of the box.
2. Cut several circles the size of the beverage can indents on the bottom of the box.
3. Have children paint the vendor tray.
4. Once the paint has dried, write "Cotton Candy" on the front of the tray.
5. Tie the yarn or rope through the holes in the sides of the box. The yarn or rope is worn around the neck, and the vendor's tray is held in front of the body.

Options:
• Use juice, popcorn, or candy containers with the vendor's tray. (Containers should be plastic or cardboard.)
• Provide play money for the children to use to make sales.

Book Link:
• *Millie at the Circus* by Karen Gunthorp (Doubleday)

Cotton Candy

Materials:
Coffee can (or similar-sized container), white construction paper, colored cotton balls, scissors, tape, glue, marker

Directions:
1. Trace the coffee can to make a circle for each child.
2. Draw dotted lines on the circle (as shown in the diagram below). These circles will be the cotton candy cones.
3. Children cut out the cones, fold the cones into shape, and tape.
4. Provide colored cotton balls for the children to use to stuff in the cone. The top layers are glued on to hold in place.
5. Once the glue has dried, the cotton candy can be placed in the holes in the Vendor Tray (p. 15).

Option:
• Color white cotton balls by placing a small amount of powdered tempera paint in a plastic bag with the cotton balls and shaking to coat.

Clown Shirt

Materials:
White T-shirt, nontoxic fabric paint (in assorted colors), shallow tins (for paint), sponges cut into shapes, scissors, newspaper

Directions:
1. Cut fringe around the arms and bottom of the T-shirt.
2. Lay the T-shirt flat and insert a section of the newspaper between the front and back of the shirt. This will prevent the paint from seeping through the fabric.
3. Place thin layers of nontoxic fabric paint in shallow tins.
4. Provide sponge shapes for the children to dip in the paint and decorate the shirt.
5. Once the shirt has dried, remove the inner newspaper.

Book Link:
• *Circus of Colors* by Lisa Hopp (Grosset & Dunlap)

Clown Bow Tie

Materials:
Bow Tie Pattern (p. 19), sturdy paper, pipe cleaners, shirt-size gift box, plastic spoons and bowls, tempera paint, golf balls, hole punch, scissors

Directions:
1. Trace the bow tie pattern onto sturdy paper and cut out. Make one per child.
2. Punch two holes in the center of each bow tie.
3. Demonstrate how to paint the bow tie. Put one bow tie in the lid of the gift box and spoon golf balls dipped in tempera paint on top of the bow tie. Tip the sides of the box back and forth to roll the balls. Children should repeat this step for each color of paint desired. Give each child a turn to decorate a tie.
4. Once the paint has dried, tie pipe cleaners through the holes in the center of each bow tie. The loose ends of the ties can be gently fastened around the child's neck.

Book Link:
• *Clifford at the Circus* by Norman Bridwell (Scholastic)

Bow Tie Pattern

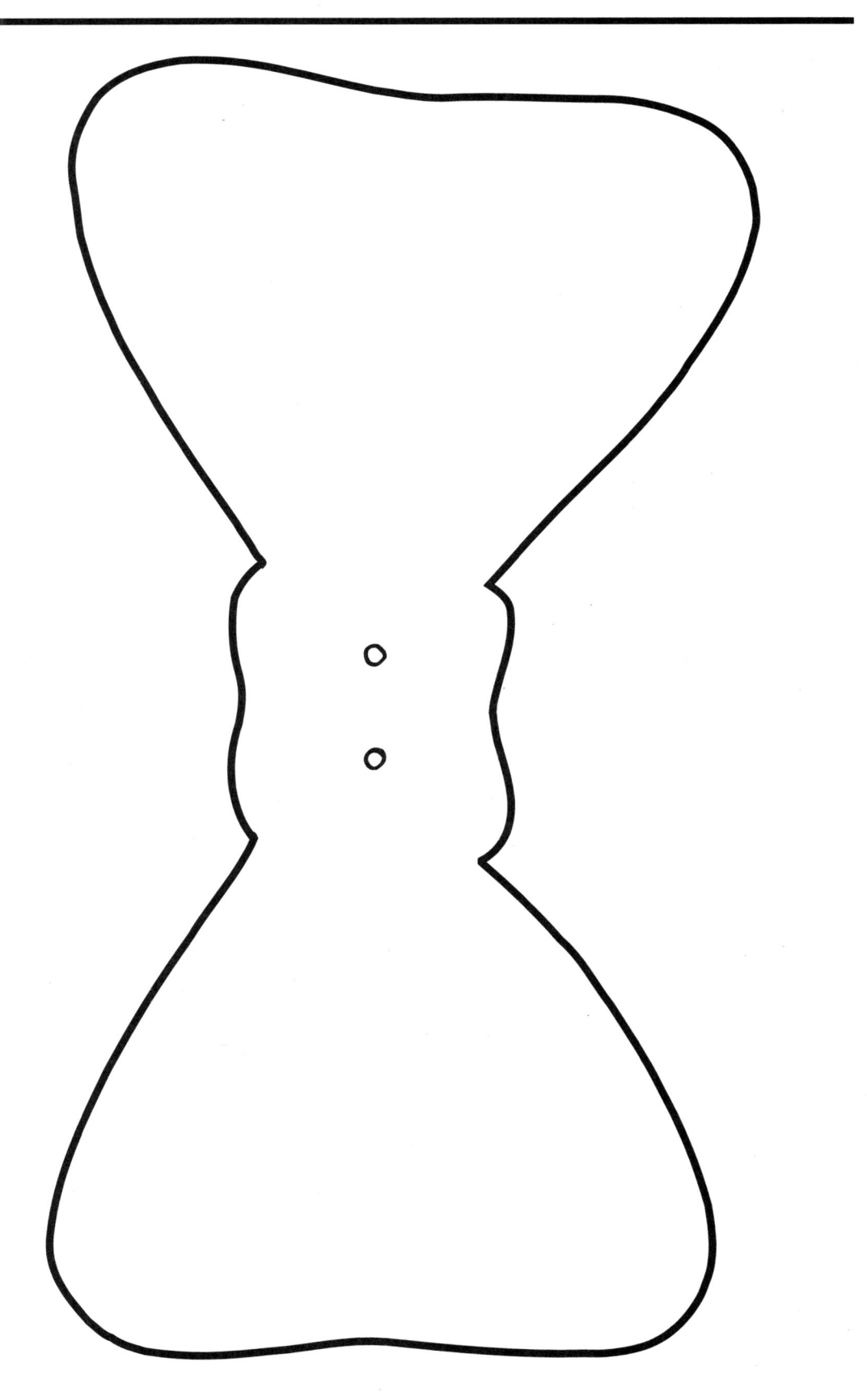

19

Clown Hat

Materials:
Old file folder (one per child), self-sticking dots (in assorted colors), colored cotton balls, glue stick, masking tape, marker, scissors, hole punch, elastic

Directions:
1. Draw a large half circle on the fold of each file folder.
2. Place a dot in the middle of the fold on each folder.

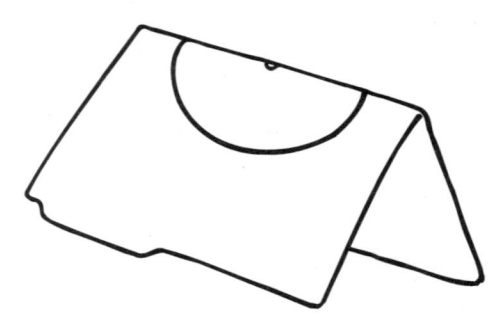

3. Keeping the file folders folded, have the children cut out the half circles.
4. Let the children open up the half circles, and cut up the fold to the dot.
5. The children shape the circles into hats and tape.
6. Provide self-sticking dots, cotton balls, and glue sticks for the children to use to decorate the clown hats.
7. Punch a hole on two sides of each hat and tie elastic through the holes. The elastic is placed under the child's chin.

Tightrope Walker Pole

Materials:
Wrapping paper tube, markers, crepe or tissue paper (in assorted colors), scissors, transparent tape, masking tape

Directions:
1. Have children decorate the tube with markers.
2. The children cut strips of crepe or tissue paper to tape to both ends of the tube.
3. Place a long strip of masking tape on the floor for the tightrope.

Book Links:
• *Angelina at the Fair* by Katherine Holabird (Clarkson N. Potter)

Tightrope Wristbands

Materials:
Toilet tissue tubes (one per child), aluminum foil, scissors, glue, paintbrushes, shallow tins (for glue), sequins

Directions:
1. Cut the toilet tissue tube in half and cut each half open. (Make two wristbands per child.)
2. Cut aluminum foil pieces large enough to completely cover a half toilet tissue tube.
3. Have children wrap the aluminum foil around the tubes.
4. Provide glue for children to brush onto the wristbands and decorate with sequins.

Tightrope Walker Hat

Materials:
Shiny bulletin board border, colored feathers, masking tape, toilet tissue tubes (one per child), glue, scissors

Directions:
1. Cut a section of bulletin board border long enough to fit around a child's head. (Make one per child.)
2. Flatten the toilet tissue tube and cut out a triangle. (Make one per child.)
3. Tape the pointed end of the triangle to the inside of the headband according to the diagram below. (The triangle may curl slightly.)

4. Provide feathers for the children to glue to the triangle.
5. Once the glue has dried, measure a headband to each child's head, and tape the ends of the band together.

Ringmaster Vest

Materials:
Paper grocery bag (one per child), black tempera paint, sponge brushes, shallow tins (for paint), rickrack (gold, silver, and white), markers, scissors, glue

Directions:
1. Cut each bag up the front of one side, and continue cutting a circle on the top of the bag.
2. Cut a circle on both narrow sides of each bag for arms, then turn the bag inside out.
3. Draw a line on the bottom of the bag, and have the children cut to the line for fringe.
4. Children sponge paint the vests black.
5. Once the vests dry, children can glue on rickrack.

Book Link:
• *If I Ran the Circus* by Dr. Seuss (Random House)

Ringmaster Hat

Materials:
Large sturdy paper plate (one per child), sturdy paper, black tempera paint, paintbrushes, shallow tins (for paint), scissors, stapler, tape, star stickers (gold and silver)

Directions:
1. Cut sturdy paper into 6 in (15 cm) wide strips. The strips should be long enough to fit around a child's head. (Make one strip per child.)
2. Cut out the center portion of each paper plate (as shown). (Make one per child.)

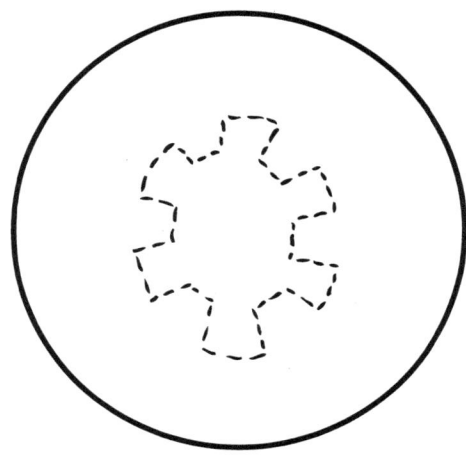

3. Fold the flaps under the paper plates and staple the strips to the flaps.
4. On each hat, tape the two ends of the strip together.
5. Have the children paint their hats black.
6. Children can decorate their dried hats with stickers.

Book Link:
- *The 12 Circus Rings* by Seymour Chwast (Voyager)

Clown With Growing Hair

Materials:
Clown Clothes Patterns (p. 27),
individual-size plastic juice containers without lids (one per child),
empty egg shells (one per child),
potting soil, grass seed,
bowls (for potting soil and seeds),
spoons (for putting seed and soil into shells),
construction paper (in assorted colors),
markers, glue stick, glue, scissors

Directions:
1. Rinse out the juice containers.
2. Trace the clown clothes patterns onto construction paper and cut. (Make one set per child.)
3. Children can decorate the clothes with markers.
4. Have children glue the clothes to the juice containers with glue sticks.
5. Provide potting soil for the children to plant grass seed in the empty egg shells.
6. Provide markers for the children to use to give each egg shell a clown face.
7. Have children carefully glue egg shells to the juice container necks.
8. Once the grass hair has grown, children can cut it.

Book Link:
• *Spot Goes to the Circus* by Eric Hill (Putnam's Sons)

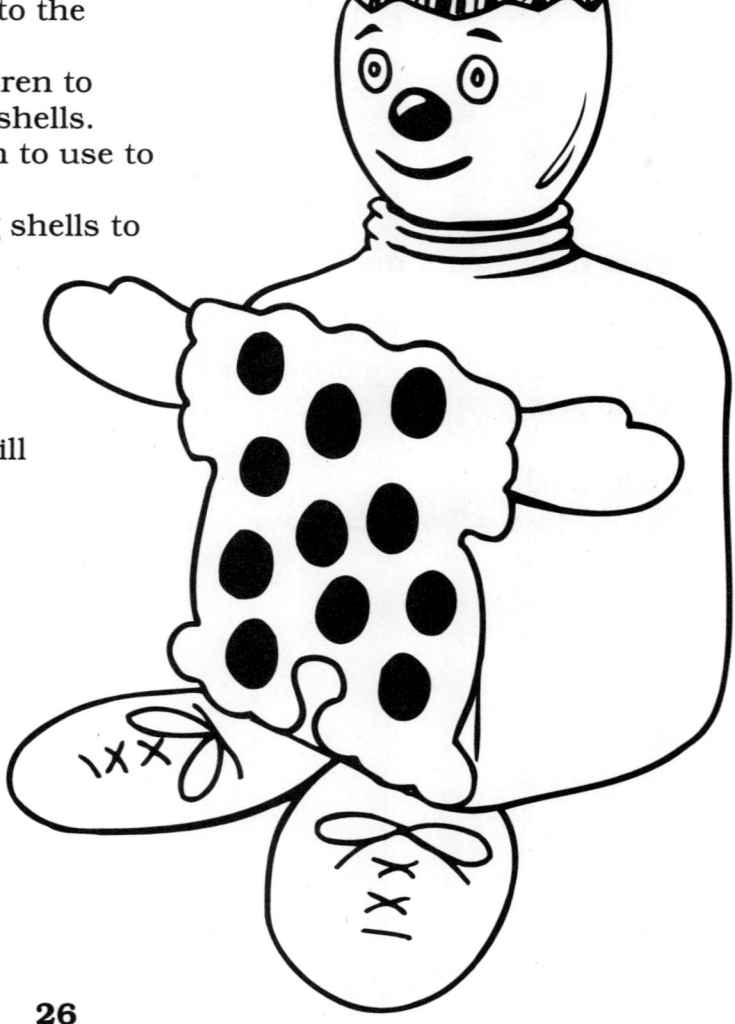

Clown Clothes Patterns

27

Elephant Puppet

Materials:
Ear and Eye Patterns (p. 29), large sturdy paper plate (one per child), sturdy paper, construction paper (blue and gray), tempera paint (black and white), shallow tins (for paint), paintbrushes, scissors, pencil, glue, gray socks (one per child), sharp instrument for cutting (for adult use only)

Directions:
1. In each paper plate, cut a hole large enough for a child's arm to fit through. (Make one per child.)
2. Trace the ear and eye patterns onto sturdy paper and cut out. These become patterns for the children to trace.
3. Provide ear and eye patterns for the children to trace onto gray and blue construction paper and cut out.
4. Have children mix black and white tempera paint to make gray.
5. Children can paint their paper plates gray.
6. Once the plates have dried, children glue the ears and eyes onto the elephants.
7. When the puppets are entirely dry, each child places a gray sock on one arm and inserts the trunk through the hole in the elephant.

Book Links:
- *I Am a Little Elephant* by Francois Crozat (Barron's)
- *Tails Toes Eyes Ears Nose* by Marilee Robin Burton (Harper Trophy)

Circus ©1998 Monday Morning Books, Inc.

Ear and Eye Patterns

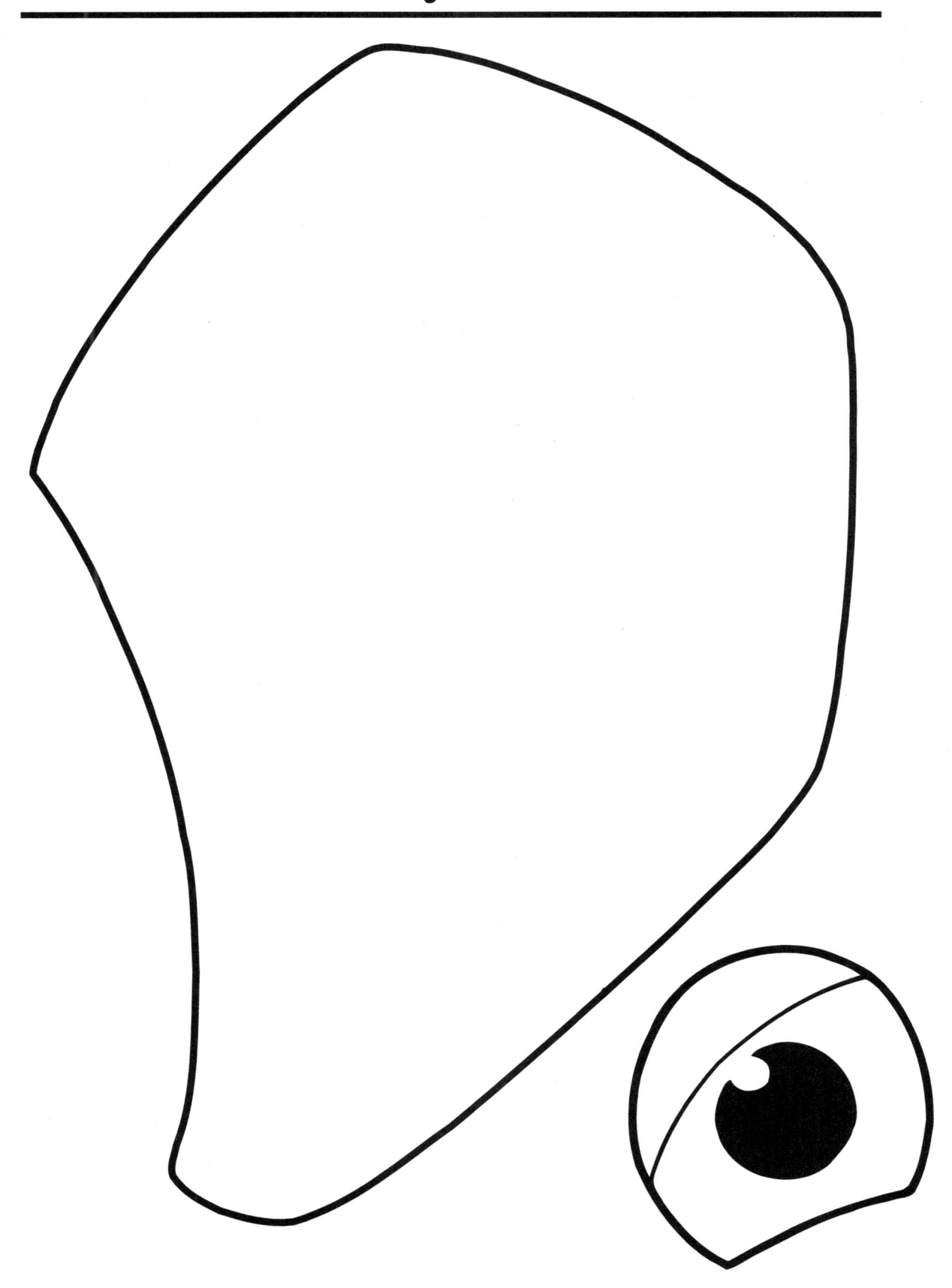

29

Paper Plate Lion Mask

Materials:
Lion Patterns (p. 32), large light-weight paper plates (one per child), sturdy paper, construction paper (brown, black, and red), yarn (brown and yellow), tempera paint (yellow), shallow tins (for paint), soap scrunchies or sponge pieces, Popsicle sticks (one per child), masking tape, scissors, glue, pencils, hole punch

Directions:
1. Cut two holes in each paper plate for eyes, and punch holes around the edge. (Make one per child.)
2. Tape a Popsicle stick handle to the back of each plate.
3. Trace the ear, nose, and tongue patterns onto sturdy paper and cut out. These patterns become templates for children to trace.
4. Cut several pieces of yarn 1 ft (31 cm) long.
5. To make loop knot manes, children fold a piece of yarn in half, insert the loop of yarn through a hole in the plate, bring the two loose ends of the yarn through the loop, and pull gently. (See diagram.) Children continue for each hole to complete the mane.
6. Provide ear, nose, and tongue patterns for the children to trace onto black, brown, and red construction paper and cut out.
7. Have children cut strips from construction paper for the whiskers.
8. Provide yellow tempera paint and soap scrunchies or sponge pieces for the children to use to paint the plates.
9. Children glue the facial features onto the lions.

Book Link:
- *Dandelion* by Don Freeman (The Viking Press)

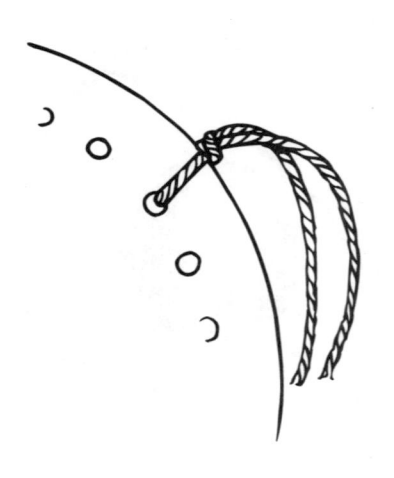

Paper Bag Tiger Puppet

Materials:
Tiger Patterns (p. 32), lunch-size paper bags (one per child), sturdy paper, construction paper (black, blue, and red), tempera paint (orange), shallow tins (for paint), paint rollers, crayons (white or yellow), scissors, glue

Directions:
1. Trace eye, ear, nose, and tongue patterns on sturdy paper and cut out. These become templates for the children to trace.
2. Have children trace the patterns onto colored construction paper and cut out.
3. Children cut strips of black construction paper for the whiskers and stripes.
4. Have children roller paint the paper bags orange.
5. Children glue the facial features on the bottom section of the bags. They can glue the stripes where desired.

Book Links:
- *I Am a Little Tiger* by Francois Crozat (Barron's)
- *A New Home for Tiger* by Joan Stimson (Barron's)
- *Tickling Tigers* by Anna Currey (Barron's)

Lion and Tiger Patterns

Dancing Bear and Stand

Materials for Dancing Bear:
Body Pattern (p. 34), Arm and Leg Patterns (p. 35) construction paper (brown, black, or white), markers, scissors, hole punch, brads

Directions for Dancing Bear:
1. Trace the body pattern onto construction paper and mark the dots. (Make one body pattern per child.)
2. Trace the arm and leg patterns onto construction paper and cut out. (Make one set per child.)
3. Have children cut out the body patterns.
4. Provide a hole punch for the children to use to punch holes through the dots.
5. Provide brads for children to use to attach the arms and legs to the bears' bodies.
6. Children can use markers to add details.

Materials for Stand:
Quart (liter) size ice cream container (one per child), stickers, sharp instrument for cutting (for adult use only)

Directions for Stand:
1. Cut a slit in the bottom of the ice cream container large enough for the bear to sit in. (Do this for each child's container.)
2. Provide stickers for the children to use to decorate the stands.

Book Links:
- *I Am a Little Bear* by Francois Crozat (Barron's)
- *Better Not Get Wet, Jesse Bear* by Nancy White Carlstrom (Aladdin)
- *The Bear Under the Stairs* by Helen Cooper (Puffin)

Body Pattern

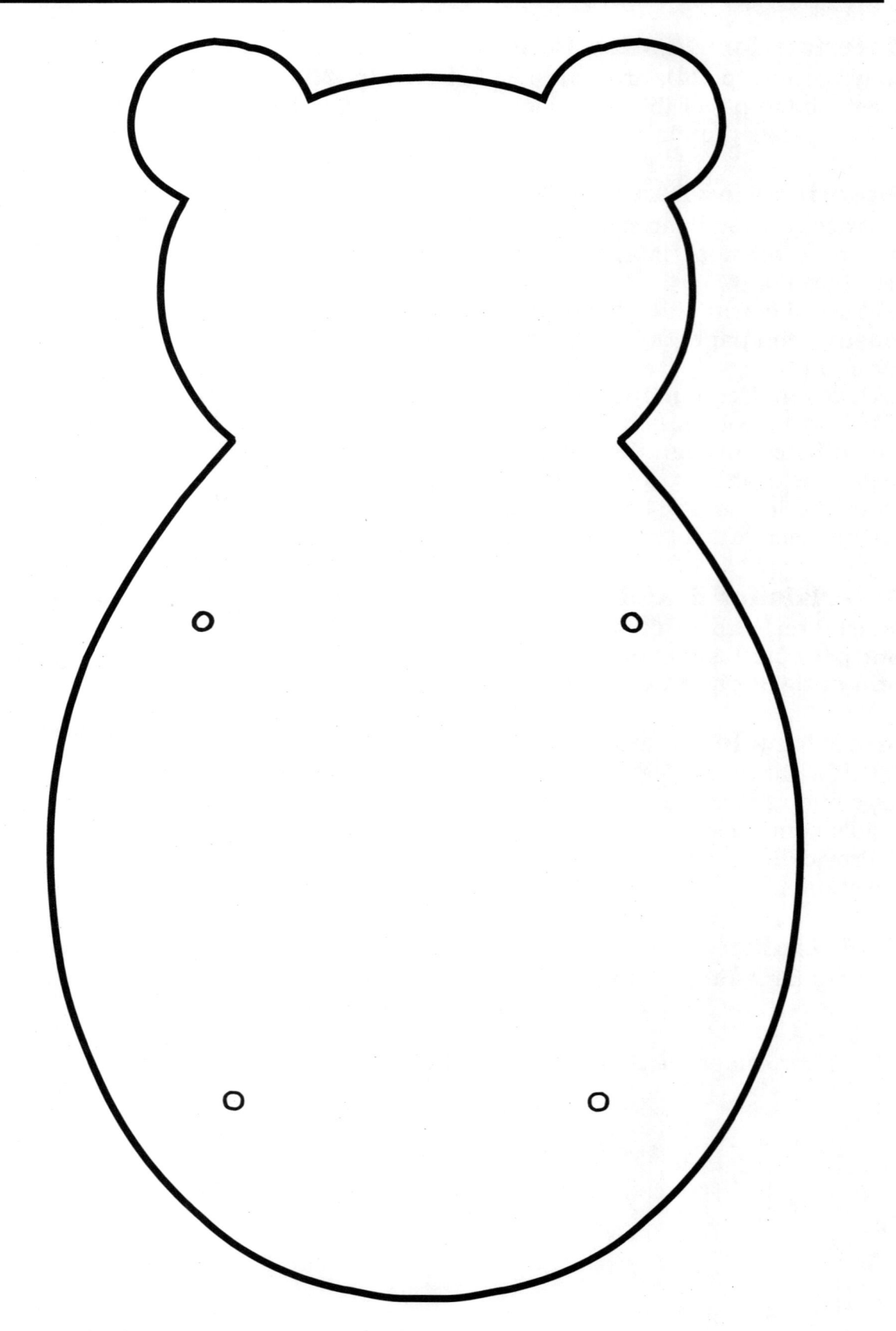

34

Arm and Leg Patterns

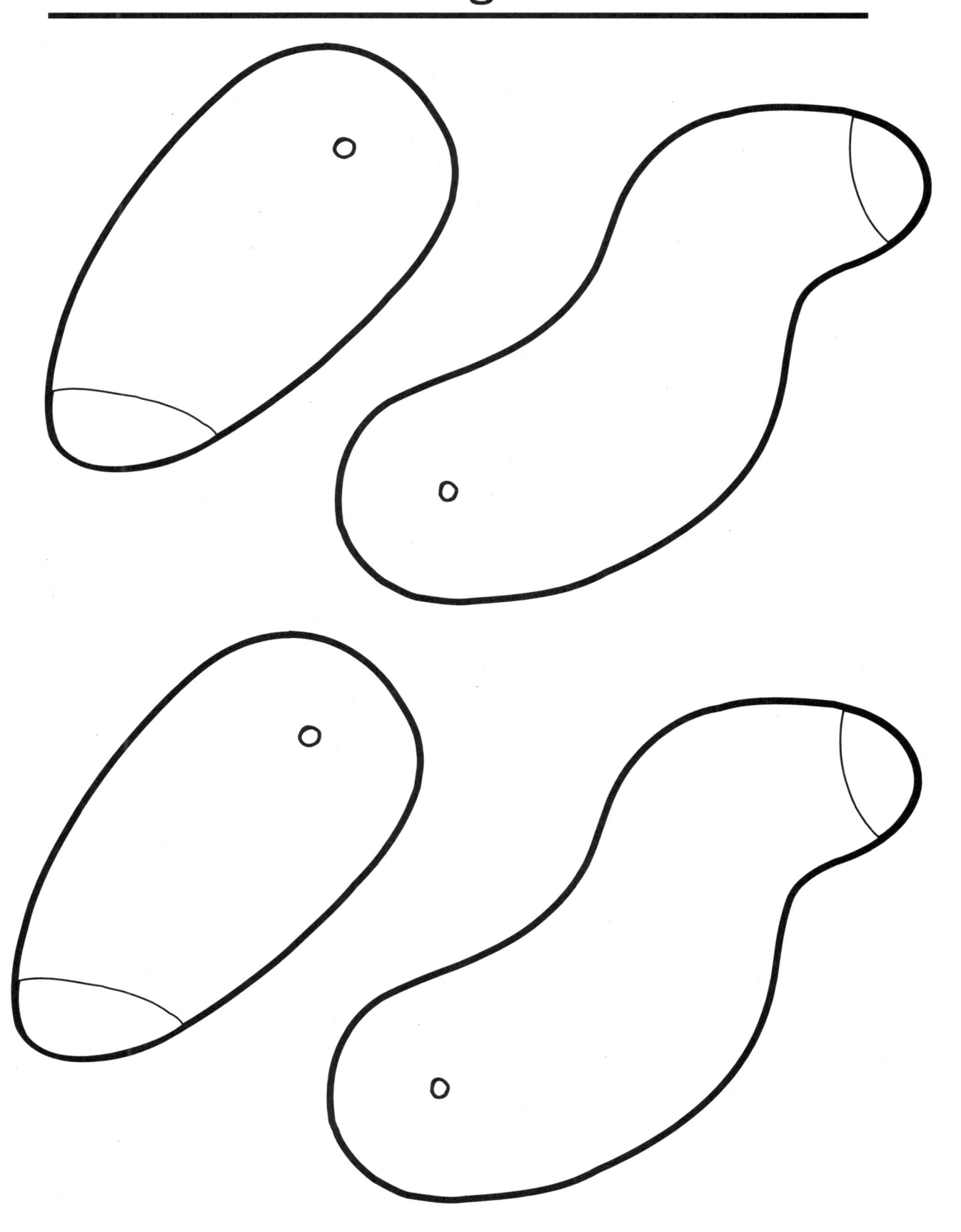

Counting Circus Bears

Materials:
Circus Bear Game Cards (p. 37), Game Board Pattern (pp. 38-39), markers or colored pencils, tape

Directions:
1. Duplicate a copy of the game board pattern, attach using tape, and color.
2. Laminate the game board.
3. Duplicate the game card pieces, color, and cut apart. Laminate and cut apart again, leaving a thin laminate border to prevent peeling.
4. Children count the dots on the game board and match the numeral cards to the corresponding dots on the game board.

Option:
- Use clear contact paper instead of laminating.

Circus Bear Game Cards

37

Game Board Pattern

Game Board Pattern

Circus Playdough

Materials:
Playdough ingredients (see recipe below), bowl, cookie cutters, rolling pins, blunt-edged plastic knives, buttons, colored macaroni, toothpicks, colored pipe cleaners, feathers

Directions:
1. Make several different colors of fluorescent dough with the children, using caution when adding the boiling water.
2. Children can create circus animals and characters out of the playdough.

Playdough Recipe:
4 cups (1 kilogram) flour
2 cups (.5 kilograms) salt
8 tsp. (40 grams) cream of tartar
10 tsp. (50 ml) liquid vegetable oil
4 cups (1 liter) boiling water
fluorescent tempera paint (desired colors)

Directions:
1. Combine the first four ingredients in a large bowl.
2. Add fluorescent paint to the boiling water.
3. Pour the water into the dry ingredients and mix.
4. Remove the dough from the bowl and knead on a floured surface.

Circus Flannel Board

Materials:
Flannel Board Patterns (p. 42), flannel board, felt (in assorted colors), scissors

Directions:
1. Trace the flannel board patterns onto felt and cut out.
2. Place the three different animals on the flannel board while the children are watching.
3. Have the children close their eyes while you change the sequence of the animals.
4. Have the children open their eyes and try to guess the original sequence of the animals.
5. Repeat this process several times.

Option:
• Sequencing can be done using the same animal with different colors or the same animal with different sizes.

Book Link:
• *The A to Z Beastly Jamboree* by Robert Bender (Lodestar Books)

Flannel Board Patterns

Clown Matching Activity

Materials:
Clown Activity Pattern (p. 44), Size and Shape Patterns (below), construction paper (in assorted colors), crayons or markers, glue stick, scissors

Directions:
1. Duplicate a copy of the size and shape patterns (below) and cut out.
2. Trace the patterns onto assorted colors of construction paper and cut out. (Use a variety of colors for each size and shape.)
3. Duplicate a copy of the clown activity pattern for each child.
4. Have children match the patterns by size and shape and glue them onto the clown activity patterns.
5. Children can use crayons or markers to decorate the patterns.

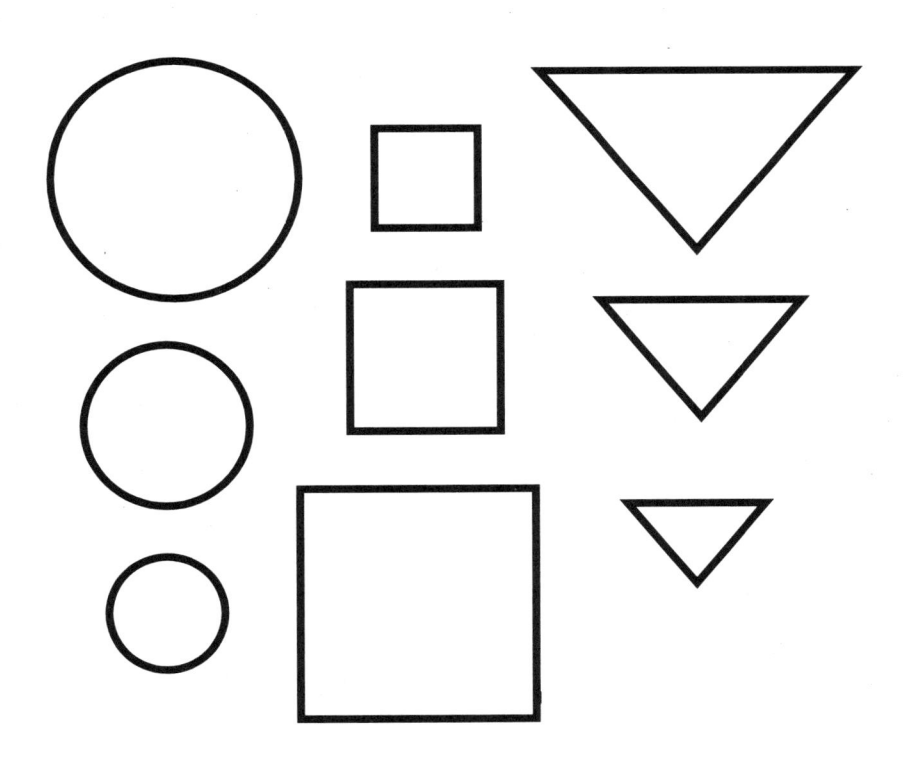

Clown Activity Pattern

Circus Puzzle

Materials:
Circus Puzzle (p. 46), plain paper, scissors, glue or glue sticks, crayons or markers, envelopes (optional)

Directions:
1. Duplicate one copy of the circus puzzle for each child.
2. Let the children color their puzzles and cut them apart on the dotted lines.
3. Children can either glue the puzzle pieces onto plain paper backgrounds, or they can store the puzzle pieces in envelopes to play with on other days.

Circus Puzzle

Circus Memory Match

Materials:
Circus Patterns (p. 48), colored markers, scissors, clear contact paper

Directions:
1. Duplicate the circus patterns twice, color, cut apart, cover with contact paper or laminate, and cut out again. (Leave a thin laminate border around each pattern to help prevent peeling.)
2. Shuffle the cards and spread them face down on a table.
3. Demonstrate how to play the game. The object is to match the circus patterns by turning the cards over two at a time. If a match is made, the cards remain face up and the child takes another turn. If a match isn't made, the cards are turned over and the next child takes a turn. Game continues until all cards are face up.

Option:
• Introduce the game by leaving the shuffled cards face up and having the children simply match the circus patterns together.

Circus Patterns

48